Lett

MW01098760

SCHOOL PUBLISHERS

Photos:
p. 2, © Harcourt Telescope; p. 3, © Superstock; p. 4, © Harcourt Telescope; p. 5, © Superstock; p. 6, © Harcourt Telescope; p. 7, © Veer; p. 8,© Corbis.

Printed in China

ISBN 10: 0-15-358375-4
ISBN 13: 978-0-15-358375-9

Ordering Options
ISBN 10: 0-15-358355-X (Grade K Below-Level Collection)
ISBN 13: 978-0-15-358355-1 (Grade K Below-Level Collection)
ISBN 10: 0-15-360628-2 (package of 5)
ISBN 13: 978-0-15-360628-1 (package of 5)

4 5 6 7 8 9 10 0940 15 14 13 12 11 10 09

pot

mop

top

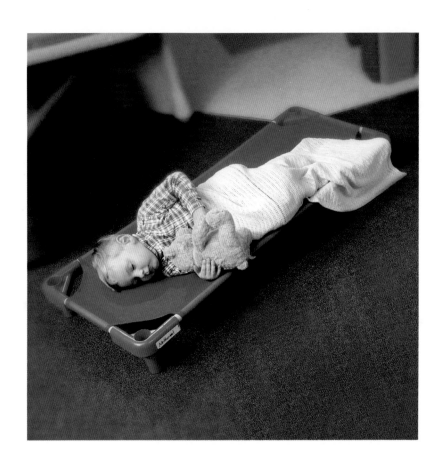

cot

hot

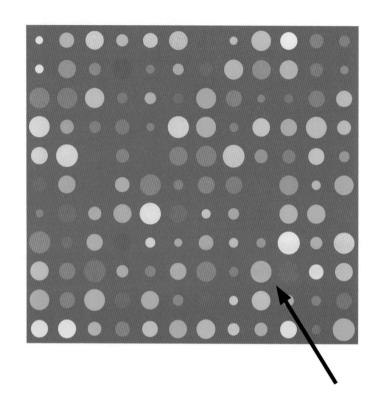

dot

hop